Come Together
synago
Calm in the Storm
By Karen Kluever
A Gathering
AF571772
Assemble
Take in

© 2002 by Abingdon Press
All rights reserved.

No part of this work may be reproduced or transmitted in any form or by any means, electronic or mechanical, including photocopying and recording, or by any information storage or retrieval system, except as may be expressly permitted by the 1976 Copyright Act or in writing by the publisher. For some material permission to photocopy is granted on the page. Requests for permission should be addressed to Permissions Office, 201 Eighth Avenue, South, P.O. Box 801, Nashville, TN 37202-0801. You may fax your request to 615-749-6128.

Cover Design: Keely Moore

Scripture Credits

Contemporary English Version (CEV)
Scripture quotations marked (CEV) are from the Contemporary English Version copyright © 1991, 1992, 1995 by American Bible Society. Used by permission.

The Message (Message)
Scripture taken from THE MESSAGE. Copyright © Eugene H. Peterson, 1993, 1994, 1995. Used by permission of NavPress Publishing Group.

New Century Version (NCV)
Scriptures quoted from The Holy Bible, New Century Version, copyright © 1987, 1988, 1991 by Word Publishing, Nashville, Tennessee 37214. Used by permission.

New International Version (NIV)
Scripture quotations marked (NIV) are taken from the HOLY BIBLE, NEW INTERNATIONAL VERSION® NIV®. Copyright © 1973, 1978, 1984 by International Bible Society. Used by permission of Zondervan Publishing House. All rights reserved.

New Revised Standard Version (NRSV)
New Revised Standard Version of the Bible, copyright 1989, Divisions of Christian Education of the National Council of Churches of Christ in the United States of America. Used by permission. All rights reserved.

02 03 04 05 06 07 08 09 10 11—10 9 8 7 6 5 4 3 2 1

Contents

Benefits for You

BE-COMING A SMALL GROUP MEMBER

As a member of a small group, you can

- be with your friends and make new ones
- be yourself
- be encouraged
- be an explorer—of the Christian faith and the Bible
- be listened to
- be able to share thoughts, opinions, and feelings with peers
- be safe—everything's confidential!
- be introduced to a caring, Christian adult who's also a group member
- be challenged to live out new insights as part of a faith community
- be responsible—for caring for others, being open-minded, keeping confidences, and inviting friends
- be valued as a child of God!

Multiplying the Benefits

GOING AND GROWING

A small group isn't a clique. It is open, inviting, and welcoming.

A small group grows as its members invite their friends. (Why would you keep such a great experience all to yourself? You've got to share it with others!)

When your small group gets to ten regular members, you'll want to "multiply" into two smaller groups. Think about it. If a small group grows and gets bigger and bigger, it's no longer a small, intimate group.

Although going, or "growing," from one group to two can be hard (people you've become close to may be in a different group), there are major benefits to multiplying:

- There's more time for everyone to participate in smaller groups; it's easier to start and end on time.
- Shy students are more likely to open up in a group of five than in a group of twelve.
- You can invite more friends, because you have room to grow.
- There's an opportunity for two more students to become group leaders; as groups multiplying, new leaders are needed.

As a small group member, you should want your group to grow. Being in a small group is a great experience and one you'll want to share with friends and other students who need a place to feel accepted and loved.

When your group is ready to multiply, plan a "birth day" celebration. Keep the small-group experience growing and going.

Purpose Statement for Student-Led Small Groups

The purposes of our small group are to

- grow closer in our relationships with God and Jesus Christ;
- grow closer in our relationships with one another;
- learn more about the Christian faith and God's Word;
- encourage honesty and sharing in an atmosphere of trust, confidentiality, and open-mindedness;
- support one another and care for one another in Christian love;
- grow in number by inviting others;
- "multiply" into two groups when we reach 10 regular members to encourage intimacy and continued growth.

Ground Rules

What's said in the group, stays in the group.

Confidentiality is critical to the small group experience.

For you and other group members to grow closer to one another and develop the special, intimate bonds of Christian friendship, you must be able to trust one another with personal information that is discussed in the group. This kind of trust is risky; but without it, no one will tell his or her true thoughts and feelings, and the group will not grow closer to one another.

Being honest requires being vulnerable, opening yourself up and exposing the real you. But you won't do this if you can't trust other group members not to spread around something you've told them. Likewise, you must keep to yourself anything of a personal nature that's shared by others in your small group. If you gossip or tell it to someone else outside the group, you break confidence, hurt someone in your group, and make your group an "unsafe" environment for others. Breaking confidentiality can be a deadly blow to a small group.

This is why confidentiality is included in the purpose statement for student-led small groups. This statement, read at the beginning of each small group session, reminds each person present to "encourage honesty and sharing in an atmosphere of trust, confidentiality, and open-mindedness."

Setting Priorities

Mary and Martha lived in Bethany, a Jerusalem suburb and frequent rest stop for Jesus on his trips to and from the city.

Luke 10:38-42 (NRSV)

Now as they went on their way, [Jesus] entered a certain village, where a woman named Martha welcomed him into her home. She had a sister named Mary, who sat at the Lord's feet and listened to what he was saying. But Martha was distracted by her many tasks; so she came to him and asked, "Lord, do you not care that my sister has left me to do all the work by myself? Tell her then to help me." But the Lord answered her, "Martha, Martha, you are worried and distracted by many things; there is need of only one thing. Mary has chosen the better part, which will not be taken away from her."

Matthew 6:33 (NRSV)

"But strive first for the kingdom of God and his righteousness, and all these things will be given to you as well."

Matthew 6:33 (KJV)

"But seek ye first the kingdom of God, and his righteousness; and all these things will be added unto you."

Martha may have been preparing a meal for at least 16 people, if Jesus disciples were with him (plus Mary, and brother Lazarus, and herself). Because of Jewish hospitality laws, Martha would have felt that all her preparations were absolutely necessary.

ingdom of God" means God's eternal and kingly rule, in this life and the next.

Notes

Pray For

Next Meeting at

____

Date

____

R & R

REFLECT AND RESPOND

Choose a translation of Matthew 6:33. Write it in the space provided. Repeat it to yourself five times at the beginning of your reflection and prayer time.

Read the text from Luke 10:38-42. Visualize the story in a modern-day setting.

- What does the house of Mary and Martha look like?
- Where are Mary and Jesus? What are they doing?
- Where is Martha? What is she doing?
- Where are Lazarus and the disciples?
- What smells are there? What are the sounds? What is the mood?

Reread the story about Mary and Martha.

- What do you think was distracting and worrying Martha?
- What distracts and worries you? Talk to God about your distractions, and ask for God's comfort, peace, and help.

Spend three minutes in prayer, asking God to guide you in setting priorities.

- What needs to become less of a priority?
- What needs to become more of a priority?
- What two things will you do to make it and keep it a priority?

"Righteousness" means "right action, acting in line with God's will."

Back to Nature

Psalm 104:1-13, 19-23, 31-33 (CEV)

I praise you, LORD God, with all my heart.
You are glorious and majestic, dressed in royal robes
and surrounded by light.
You spread out the sky like a tent,
and you built your home over the mighty ocean.
The clouds are your chariot with the wind as its wings.
The winds are your messengers,
and flames of fire are your servants.

You built foundations for the earth, and it will never be shaken.
You covered the earth with the ocean
that rose above the mountains.
Then your voice thundered!
And the water flowed down the mountains
and through the valleys to the place you prepared.
Now you have set boundaries,
so that the water will never flood the earth again.

You provide streams of water in the hills and valleys,
so that the donkeys and other wild animals
can satisfy their thirst.
Birds build their nests nearby and sing in the trees.
From your home above you send rain on the hills
and water the earth. . . .

You created the moon to tell us the seasons.
The sun knows when to set, and you made the darkness,
so the animals in the forest could come out at night.
Lions roar as they hunt for the food you provide.
But when morning comes, they return to their dens,
then we go out to work until the end of day. . . .

Our LORD, we pray that your glory will last forever
and that you will be pleased with what you have done.
You look at the earth, and it trembles.
You touch the mountains, and smoke goes up.
As long as I live,
I will sing and praise you, the LORD God.

This psalm is a hymn to the Maker and Sustainer of creation.

A "psalm" is a Hebrew poem, often written to be prayed or sung by an individual or a group.

"lames of fire" means "lightning bolts."

Notes

Pray For

Next Meeting at

____

Date

____

R & R

REFLECT AND RESPOND

Find a place where you can be alone and not be seen or heard by anyone. Read aloud the verses from Psalm 104. Read them aloud a second time, offering them as a prayer of praise to God.

Use a highlighter to mark every word in the Psalm 104 verses that refers to something God created. Then write your own prayer of thanksgiving, mentioning each item you highlighted.

Draw a picture of a person, place, or thing created by God, through which you experience God's presence or that helps you reflect on God.

List three things you can do to more faithfully protect God's creation. Be specific. Make at least one of the items something that takes some real effort and activity.

1.

2.

3.

Reread the verses from Psalm 104. Write your own psalm, song, or poem describing the things that you personally have seen or experienced in nature. Or rewrite Psalm 104, changing some of the words to make it more meaningful to you.

Forgiveness

1 John 1:8-9 (NIV)

If we claim to be without sin, we deceive ourselves and the truth is not in us. If we confess our sins, [God] is faithful and just and will forgive us our sins and purify us from all unrighteousness.

Luke 11:2-4 (NIV)

[Jesus] said to them, "When you pray, say:

" 'Father,
hallowed be your name,
your kingdom come.
Give us each day our daily bread.
Forgive us our sins,
  for we also forgive everyone who sins against us.
And lead us not into temptation.' "

Luke 17:3b-4 (CEV)

"Correct any followers of mine who sin, and forgive the ones who say they are sorry. Even if one of them mistreats you seven times in one day and says, 'I am sorry,' you should still forgive that person."

Ephesians 4:32 (NIV)

Be kind and compassionate to one another, forgiving each other, just as in Christ God forgave you.

"Sin" means "turning away from God, disobeying God's teachings or commandments."

The concept of "faithful and just" is that God's response to forgive sin comes from God's very nature and gracious commitment to us.

sus expected his followers to forgive; forgiving others is an act of obedience to m, not an ability that comes with great faith.

Notes

Pray For

Next Meeting at

____

Date

____

R & R

REFLECT AND RESPOND

Open your devotion times this week by reading the prayer in Luke 11:2-4 or pray from memory the Lord's Prayer.

Read 1 John 1:8-9. Highlight the words that are most significant to you. Reread the verse slowly, pausing to focus and reflect on each highlighted word. Make notes on the following:

- what each word means to you
- a feeling or experience you associate with the word

Think about the last 24 hours:

- List what you did, said, or thought for which you need to be forgiven. And ask God for forgiveness for each of those.
- List anyone from whom you need to ask for forgiveness.

Read Ephesians 4:32 and Luke 17:3b-4.

- Is there someone who has wronged you?

Tell God what that person did to you and how it made you feel. (You can use the space at left to write about your feelings.) If you feel that you can't forgive that person, tell God that too. Ask God to help you forgive. If forgiving is hard for you to do, repeat this conversation with God often. Over time, look for any changes in yourself, the other person, or the situation, which may indicate God's activity in helping you to forgive. Make notes on what happens.

When Boy Meets Girl

Genesis 1:27 is the first occurrence of poetry in the Hebrew Scriptures, or Old Testament, which is about 40 percent poetry.

Genesis 1:27-28a, 31 (NRSV)

So God created humankind in his image,
in the image of God he created them;
male and female he created them.
God blessed them, and God said to them, "Be fruitful and multiply, and fill the earth and subdue it." . . .

God saw everything that he had made, and indeed, it was very good.

Genesis 2:18, 20-25 (NRSV)

The LORD God said, "It is not good that the man should be alone; I will make him a helper as his partner." . . . The man gave names to all cattle, and to the birds of the air, and to every animal of the field; but for the man there was not found a helper as his partner. So the LORD God caused a deep sleep to fall upon the man, and he slept; then he took one of his ribs and closed up its place with flesh. And the rib that the LORD God had taken from the man he made into a woman and brought her to the man. Then the man said,

"This at last is bone of my bones
and flesh of my flesh;
this one shall be called Woman,
for out of Man this one was taken."

Therefore a man leaves his father and his mother and clings to his wife, and they become one flesh. And the man and his wife were both naked, and were not ashamed.

Hebrew for "man" is "adam"; Hebrew for "ground" is "adamah."

the Genesis 2 Creation story, to be created from something (woman from man, an from earth) doesn't imply subordination to it.

Notes

Pray for

Next Meeting at

____

Date

____

R & R

REFLECT AND RESPOND

Read the Scripture passages and list three truths about men and women that you believe we can learn from these passages.

Make two columns in the space at left. Label them "Regular Guy" and "Godly Guy" if you're a guy, or "Regular Girl" and "Godly Girl" if you're a girl. List three to five characteristics under each.

- Which column best describes you?
- Who or what has influenced your understanding of what it means to be a man (or woman)?
- Were these positive influences or negative ones? Explain.

Reread the first Genesis passage. Think about your being created in God's image.

- What does that mean to you?
- Are these verses encouraging, intimidating, illuminating, or irrelevant to you? Explain.

List three members of the opposite sex with whom you have some relationship (friend, romantic interest, family member, teacher). Reflect on each of these as your brother or sister in Christ.

- How would seeing them as your Christian brothers or sisters affect your relationships with them? your thoughts about them? treatment of them?

YOU + GOD + ME

I didn't think that I wanted God in my romantic relationship. It's weird to think of having three people in a relationship; but since meeting my girlfriend, I have found God to be increasingly present in my life.

Before I met her, I was in a transition period. I had been active in my church's youth program and good friends with my youth minister. When he left, the group disintegrated. I had no one to talk about God with.

My girlfriend invited me to a small group, to her youth group, and to sit with her in church. I went to all these places to see her; but instead of placing me in the small group she was leading, she put me in another group so I could not come just because she was there.

I began to feel like I had with my former youth group. I had never been in a relationship with someone who was so open about Christ. I realized I had wanted something like this all my life.

—Reid Linker, 18
Charlotte, North Carolina

As Creedence Clearwater Revival says in one of my favorite songs, "Someday Never Comes," God didn't intend for us to live each day like we knew the next day would be there. God wants us to love God today, right now, and treat others with love right now too. But it's difficult to do that with enemies, or people who have done you wrong. The last thing you want to do is tell persons who have hurt you that you love them. It's so much easier to fluff it off and say, "Maybe I'll work things out tomorrow." What if tomorrow never comes? What happens then?

Forgiving is one of the hardest things to do, but it is also one of the most noble. Some of the best friends I have are those who are quick to say, "It's okay, I know you made a mistake and I forgive you." Not only does it make me feel better to know that some of the things I do wrong are forgivable by my friends, it makes me realize that whatever I've done is forgivable by God, as long as I make amends. Forgiving someone shows a lot of humility: It keeps you off that pedestal called pride.

Forgiving is not the hardest part, though. I would say that forgetting is. As humans with amazing memories, forgetting a wrong may be impossible, but to truly forgive someone means not holding grudges. If you treat persons who have hurt you as they may deserve to be treated—poorly or without respect—then you haven't forgiven them in your heart or in God's eyes. It's hard to treat people the same after they've wronged you, but it's absolutely necessary if the friendship is going to last and if you want to remain a strong servant of God's. Besides, what if "Someday" never came and you never forgave that person? Then you would never forgive yourself.

DON'T WAIT TO FORGIVE

—Candace Lucas, 17
Charlotte, North Carolina

How Do You Score in Love?

1 Corinthians 13:4-7 (NRSV)

Love is patient; love is kind; love is not envious or boastful or arrogant or rude. It does not insist on its own way; it is not irritable or resentful; it does not rejoice in wrongdoing, but rejoices in the truth. It bears all things, believes all things, hopes all things, endures all things.

1 Corinthians 13:4-7 (The Message)

Love never gives up.
Love cares more for others than for self.
Love doesn't want what it doesn't have.
Love doesn't strut,
Doesn't have a swelled head,
Doesn't force itself on others,
Isn't always "me first,"
Doesn't fly off the handle,
Doesn't keep score of the sins of others,
Doesn't revel when others grovel,
Takes pleasure in the flowering of truth,
Puts up with anything,
Trusts God always,
Always looks for the best,
Never looks back,
But keeps going to the end.

This well-known passage on love is in a letter written by the apostle Paul to the Christian church in Corinth, a major city in Greece during the first century. Paul was concerned about problems in the Corinthian church, such as divisions, immorality, and jealousy.

Notes

Pray For

Next Meeting at

____

Date

____

R & R

REFLECT AND RESPOND

List what you want in an ideal romantic relationship. (Be honest.)

- Read 1 Corinthians 13. Compare your list to the love described in the Bible. What's similar? different?

Reread the passage from *The Message.*

- Rate yourself on each of the characteristics of love.

Draw a heart to represent one of your relationships (past, present, or future). Draw a cross to show where God is in the relationship. (If God is an important part of the relationship, draw the cross in the center of the heart. If God isn't in the picture, put the cross outside the heart.)

- How might the relationship be different if the cross were in a different place?

Give God your love life. If you are in a relationship, write the name of your boyfriend or girlfriend:

______________________________.

Pray daily for your relationship and for your boyfriend or girlfriend.

If you are not in a relationship, pray for future relationships and future boyfriends or girlfriends.

For the apostle Paul, sexual purity was a distinctive mark of the Christian community in the midst of a sexually immoral culture.

1 Corinthians 6:12-20 (CEV)

Some of you say, "We can do anything we want to." But I tell you that not everything is good for us. So I refuse to let anything have power over me. You also say, "Food is meant for our bodies, and our bodies are meant for food." But I tell you that God will destroy them both. We are not supposed to do indecent things with our bodies. We are to use them for the Lord who is in charge of our bodies. God will raise us from death by the same power that he used when he raised our Lord to life.

Don't you know that your bodies are part of the body of Christ? Is it right for me to join part of the body of Christ to a prostitute? No, it isn't! Don't you know that a man who does that becomes part of her body? The Scriptures say, "The two of them will be like one person." But anyone who is joined to the Lord is one in spirit with him.

Don't be immoral in matters of sex. That is a sin against your own body in a way that no other sin is. You surely know that your body is a temple where the Holy Spirit lives. The Spirit is in you and is a gift from God. You are no longer your own. God paid a great price for you. So use your body to honor God.

In Corinth, prostitutes were dedicated to the service of Aphrodite, the goddess of love and sex.

Notes

Pray For

Next Meeting at

____

Date

____

R & R

REFLECT AND RESPOND

Read the Bible passage, then read it again slowly. Highlight words or phrases that are significant to you. Repeat and reflect on these words and phrases. Jot down thoughts or questions you have. Listen for what God is saying to you as you "pray the Scriptures."

In the space at left, write 1 Corinthians 6:20: "God paid a great price for you. So use your body to honor God."

Take your Notebook and stand in front of a mirror. Look at yourself in the mirror and read this verse aloud five times. Say this verse to yourself every time you look in a mirror.

- What three things do you do that honor God with your body? List them at left.
- What three things do you do that dishonor God with your body? Ask for forgiveness and for God's help to stop doing things that dishonor God. Talk to God about that now.

Reflect on the price God paid for you through the death of God's Son on the cross. Reflect on God's grief and loss over the death of Jesus, and the depth of God's love for you.

- Why is sexual intimacy important to God and to our own life of faith?

Jesus, who was absolutely certain of God's goodness, wanted his followers to pray with the same confidence in God's good and loving nature.

Deuteronomy 4:7 (CEV)

(*Moses is speaking to the nation of Israel, the Hebrew people.*)

And what makes us greater than other nations? We have a God who is close to us and answers our prayers.

Matthew 7:7-8 (CEV)

"Ask, and you will receive. Search, and you will find. Knock, and the door will be opened for you. Everyone who asks will receive. Everyone who searches will find. And the door will be opened for everyone who knocks."

Romans 8:26 (CEV)

In certain ways we are weak, but the Spirit is here to help us. For example, when we don't know what to pray for, the Spirit prays for us in ways that cannot be put into words.

Of the three members of the Trinity—God, Jesus the Son, and the Holy Spirit—the Spirit is traditionally understood to be an advocate for God's people, presenting our yearnings to God when we feel too weak, inadequate, or too burdened to do it on our own.

Notes

Pray for

Next Meeting at

____

Date

____

R & R

REFLECT AND RESPOND

Read the Scripture verses on prayer. Pick one that speaks to your prayer life or one that is especially encouraging to you. Write it in the space at left. Repeat it slowly several times during the week.

Throughout the week, use the ACTS method of praying. Use the guide below by filling in the blanks. Try different words or phrases each time.

Dear God,

A You are ______________ (word/phrase of Adoration: a compliment).

C I am sorry for __________. (Confess something you've done that was wrong.)

T Thank you for __________________________.

S Please help ______________ (a Special Request for yourself or others). Amen.

Write an e-mail to God. Use the space below or at the left or print one to stick in your Notebook. What would you say to God? ask God? unload on God? Be honest and real.

From:

To:

Subject:

- How would God reply? What does God say to you? What do you need to hear God say?

For the Hebrew (Jewish) people, the Sabbath is the seventh day of the week, from sunset on Friday to sunset on Saturday. Traditionally, it is their day for worship and for resting from work, in obedience to the third commandment.

Exodus 20:8-11 (NRSV)

Remember the sabbath day, and keep it holy. Six days you shall labor and do all your work. But the seventh day is a sabbath to the LORD your God; you shall not do any work—you, your son or your daughter, your male or female slave, your livestock, or the alien resident in your towns. For in six days the LORD made heaven and earth, the sea, and all that is in them, but rested the seventh day; therefore the LORD blessed the sabbath day and consecrated it.

Psalm 149:1-4 (NRSV)

Praise the LORD!
Sing to the LORD a new song,
his praise in the assembly of the faithful.
Let Israel be glad in its Maker;
let the children of Zion rejoice in their King.
Let them praise his name with dancing,
making melody to him with tambourine and lyre.
For the LORD takes pleasure in his people;
he adorns the humble with victory.

A lyre is a stringed, musical instrument of the harp family having two curved arms connected at the upper end by a crossbar, used to accompany a singer or reciter of poetry, especially in ancient Greece.

Jesus was Jewish, so he would have observed the Sabbath. He also retreated from time to time to places where he could be alone and refresh his body and soul.

Consecrated" means "set apart as sacred; declared holy."

5:7). Over time, "Zion" was used to refer to Jerusalem as the Hebrew (Israelite) religious capital and, eventually, to the entire nation of Israel.

Notes

Pray For

Next Meeting at

____

Date

____

"Holy" means "dedicated to God."

R & R

REFLECT AND RESPOND

Describe your current Sabbath experience (Sunday or other day):

___ Don't really have one

___ Forced and frustrating

___ Familiar and routine but less than satisfying

___ Pretty good; no complaints

___ A real spiritual "boost"—wouldn't miss it!

List three things you can do to create a more meaningful, or holy, Sabbath day. (Ask God for help with this.) Promise yourself and God to do them regularly.

Read Psalm 149:1-4. Imagine that you are a part of this Temple worship service. How many people are there? What do you hear? Do you smell incense burning? What is the mood? Can you imagine music and dancing? the passion and joy that fills them? What is the spirit of the worship? Worship can be private or public, quiet and reverent, or loud and joyful.

- What is one way you can privately worship during your week?
- Do you worship God publicly in a church? If not, find a church that offers worship that is meaningful to you. Check it out on your own or go with friends who like their worship service. If your church offers a meaningful worship, invite friends who are searching to go with you.

Devotional

THE COMFORT OF PRAYER

I have a friend, Megan, who has not been raised in a Christian environment. Last year, she and I lost a close friend to suicide. The only way I was surviving was through prayer; and as open-minded as I tried to be, I knew that Megan wasn't doing well. I was so worried that I confronted her.

Megan told me that she was uncomfortable praying to God, but that didn't stop her from praying altogether. She talks to the stars. Lying underneath a night sky, she speaks to the lights above her. I asked Megan if she thought that she was talking only to gases up in the universe. She thought a moment and said that she knew she was really talking to God.

Sometimes when I pray, I think about Megan and her stars. I'm so thankful that I have a close relationship with God, because that relationship always gives me someone to run to. It's comforting to know that we are not alone; and even for people who haven't found that light in their life yet, at least they know that there's something. If Megan taught me anything, she taught me that prayer is a powerful thing. Even those without faith can believe in its abilities.

—Erin Farney, 17
Charlotte, North Carolina

One Friday night, my friends and I were looking for something to do. We wanted to go to a party that we knew our parents wouldn't let us go to. My friends told their parents that they were going to my house, and I told my mom that I was going to one of my friends'. We met and went to the party, knowing that our parents had told us not to and that we had lied to them.

We had so much fun at the party that we lost track of time and went well past curfew. We didn't know what we were going to say to our parents. When we got home, all of our parents knew that something was up, because they had all called one another, trying to find out where we were. So now, not only were we late, but we were caught too.

Although one of my friends never admitted to lying about his whereabouts, the rest of us did the right thing and confessed.

—Ross Brewer, 15
Charlotte, North Carolina

COMING CLEAN

The crowd listening to Jesus would have understood that "the eye of a needle" referred to one of the gates of Jerusalem, which was very difficult for camels to get through, due to their size.

Luke 18:18-27 (The Message)

One day one of the local officials asked him, "Good teacher, what must I do to deserve eternal life?"

Jesus said, "Why are you calling me good? No one is good—only God. You know the commandments, don't you? No illicit sex, no killing, no stealing, no lying, honor your father and mother."

He said, "I've kept them all for as long as I can remember."

When Jesus heard that, he said, "Then there's only one thing left to do: Sell everything you own and give it away to the poor. You will have riches in heaven. Then come, follow me."

That was the last thing the official expected to hear. He was very rich and became terribly sad. He was holding on tight to a lot of things and not about to let them go.

Seeing his reaction, Jesus said, "Do you have any idea how difficult it is for people who have it all to enter God's kingdom? I'd say it's easier to thread a camel through a needle's eye than get a rich person into God's kingdom."

"Then who has a chance at all?" the others asked.

"No chance at all," Jesus said, "if you think you can pull it off by yourself. Every chance in the world if you trust God to do it."

Luke 18:28-30 (CEV)

Peter said, "Remember, we left everything to be your followers."

Jesus answered, "You can be sure that anyone who gives up home or wife or brothers or family or children because of God's kingdom, will be given much more in this life. And in the future world they will have eternal life."

"No one is good—only God." Jesus' point is that goodness isn't based on merit; you aren't good because of the things you do. The source of all goodness is God. Following the commandments, or "doing good," should be an expression of faith, not a way to "score points."

Notes

Pray for

Next Meeting at

____

Date

____

R & R

REFLECT AND RESPOND

Read the Scripture passages and then read them again slowly. Imagine the scene occurring in your school:

- Who would be in the role of the wealthy official? (Think of someone who is well off and has a lot of status at school.) What is this person's attitude before, during, and after his or her conversation with Jesus? What happens to him or her after that conversation?
- Imagine yourself in the crowd, hanging out and with Jesus. How do you react to his words?

Make a list of your things and estimate their total value.

- Are you satisfied with what you have? Why, or why not?
- Do you have too much? How much is too much? If you have too much, what will you do about it?

Write your answers to these questions in the space at left:

- In what ways are you like the wealthy person in the story? unlike?
- Do you think that "being good" and "following the rules" is what Jesus wants from you?
- What might Jesus be calling you to "leave behind" to follow him?
- How do things keep you from loving and honoring God? others? Talk to God about this.

Sweet Temptations: Revenge

Luke 6:27-36 (CEV)

(*Jesus is speaking to a large group of his followers.*)

"This is what I say to all who will listen to me:

"Love your enemies, and be good to everyone who hates you. Ask God to bless anyone who curses you, and pray for everyone who is cruel to you. If someone slaps you on one cheek, don't stop that person from slapping you on the other cheek. If someone wants to take your coat, don't try to keep back your shirt. Give to everyone who asks and don't ask people to return what they have taken from you. Treat others just as you want to be treated.

"If you love only someone who loves you, will God praise you for that? Even sinners love people who love them. If you are kind only to someone who is kind to you, will God be pleased with you for that? Even sinners are kind to people who are kind to them. If you lend money only to someone you think will pay you back, will God be pleased with you for that? Even sinners lend to sinners because they think they will get it all back.

"But love your enemies and be good to them. Lend without expecting to be paid back. Then you will get a great reward, and you will be the true children of God in heaven. He is good even to people who are unthankful and cruel. Have pity on others, just as your Father has pity on you."

Luke 6:31 (NRSV)

"Do to others as you would have them do to you."

This text is part of a larger passage known as Luke's "Sermon on the Plain," because it begins with a reference to Jesus' speaking on "a level place" (Luke 6:17). Many of Jesus' teachings in this text parallel those in "The Sermon on the Mount," in the Book of Matthew.

Jesus doesn't want us to behave the same way as those who mistreat us do—by getting even. Rather, we are to imitate God's behavior, which good and compassionate, even to those who are undeserving.

Notes

Pray For

Next Meeting at

____

Date

____

R & R

REFLECT AND RESPOND

Read the Bible passage. Highlight what you think are the most important words and phrases. In the space at the left, copy a sentence or phrase to focus on this week.

Make a list of people you consider to be enemies—people who hate you or want to harm you (physically, emotionally, spiritually, financially, or socially). The enemy doesn't have to be someone you know personally; the enemy could be a group or a type of person.

- How do you define *enemy*?
- Was this list shorter or longer than you expected?
- Pray for those on your list.

Reread the Bible passage. Then read aloud the second paragraph, beginning with "Love your enemies." At the beginning of each sentence, say your own name, as if Jesus were making each statement directly to you.

- Which statement is the most difficult for you to do? Ask God for help.

Think of one particular person whom you consider to be an enemy. Write the person's name.

- What can you do in this situation that would distinguish you as a Christian, one who believes in and follows the teachings of Jesus Christ?
- Pray for this person.

Sweet Temptations: Deceit

Exodus 20:16 (NIV)

"You shall not give false testimony against your neighbor."

Mark 7:20-23 (CEV)

Then Jesus said:

"What comes from your heart is what makes you unclean. Out of your heart come evil thoughts, vulgar deeds, stealing, murder, unfaithfulness in marriage, greed, meanness, deceit, indecency, envy, insults, pride, and foolishness. All of these come from your heart, and they are what make you unfit to worship God."

Ephesians 4:15 (CEV)

Love should always make us tell the truth. Then we will grow in every way and be more like Christ.

This verse comes from Paul's letter to the Christian church in Ephesus, the most important city in an area that is now Turkey. Paul encouraged these early Christians in their faithful pursuit to grow into the likeness of Jesus Christ and in their unity as members of the body of Christ, the church.

Exodus 20:16 is one of the Ten Commandments, God's rules for how the Hebrew people should relate to God and to one another. The Ten Commandments spelled out what was right and wrong and what pleased and did not please God.

In Jesus' day, the Jewish people observed certain religious laws to mak sure that they were acceptable to worship God, or "clean." A person w considered "unclean," or unacceptable to God, if he or she had certair kinds of diseases or broke certain laws by touching or eating things considered "unclean." Becoming "clean" again sometimes required a certain ceremony, such as a ritual cleansing or offering an animal sacrifice.

False testimony" is "making an incorrect or deceitful statement or declaration gainst another person."

one keeps the Law by following the spirit of the Law or by keeping it with one's heart, not just "going through the motions" and following the "letter" of the Law. It's what is in your heart that is the source of either the sinful (unacceptable) or the loving (acceptable) things you do.

Notes

Pray for

Next Meeting at

____

Date

____

R & R

REFLECT AND RESPOND

Read the Bible verses. Circle one you will repeat and pray about at the beginning of your personal devotional times.

Think about how honest or dishonest you are in your life.

- How important is it for you to be honest?
- What people or situations have had the greatest influence on your attitude about or practice of honesty?

Reread Mark 7:20-23.

- Based on your experience and reason, do you agree with Jesus' statement? Why, or why not?
- Which of the "unclean" activities listed by Jesus do you see evident in your own attitudes and actions?
- "Unclean" or sinful activities, such as deceit, may make you feel distant from God or unworthy of being close to God. If you desire to draw closer to God, confess those sins to God and ask God's help not to do them anymore. God loves you and wants a close relationship with you. God will forgive you and help you keep from doing those things that harm your relationship with God.

Reread Ephesians 4:15.

- Why is it important for members of a small group, youth group, or church) to be honest with one another? with people outside the faith community?

For the Jews of Joseph's day, to be engaged to someone was a form of marriage. (An engaged woman would be referred to as her fiancé's "wife.") Although a couple didn't live together while they were engaged, a divorce would have been needed to break their relationship.

Matthew 1:18-21, 24 (Your Bible)

Matthew 3:1-2, 6, 13-15 (The Message)

While Jesus was living in the Galilean hills, John, called "the Baptizer," was preaching in the desert country of Judea. His message was simple and austere, like his desert surroundings: "Change your life. God's kingdom is here." . . .

There at the Jordan River those who came to confess their sins were baptized into a changed life. . . .

Jesus then appeared. . . . He wanted John to baptize him. John objected, "I'm the one who needs to be baptized, not *you*!"

But Jesus insisted. "Do it. God's work, putting things right all these centuries, is coming together right now in this baptism." So John did it.

Matthew 4:23-24 (The Message)

[Jesus] went all over Galilee. He used synagogues for meeting places and taught people the truth of God. God's kingdom was his theme—that beginning right now they were under God's government, a good government! He also healed people of their diseases and of the bad effects of their bad lives. Word got around the entire Roman province of Syria. People brought anybody with an ailment, whether mental, emotional, or physical. Jesus healed them, one and all. More and more people came, the momentum gathering.

Matthew 16:13-17 (The Message)

[Jesus] asked his disciples, "What are people saying about who the Son of Man is?"

They replied, "Some think he is John the Baptizer, some say Elijah, some Jeremiah or one of the other prophets."

He pressed them, "And how about you? Who do you say I am?"

Simon Peter said, "You're the Christ, the Messiah, the Son of the living God."

Jesus came back, "God bless you Simon! . . . You didn't get that answer out of books or from teachers. My Father in heaven, God himself, let you in on this secret of who I really am."

Matthew 28:1-6 (Your Bible)

aptism symbolized spiritual cleansing in Jesus' day (and still does today).

child who was not her husband's.

Notes

Pray for

Next Meeting at

____

Date

____

R & R

REFLECT AND RESPOND

Read the book of Matthew during the next week. (Read four chapters a day from a translation that is easy to understand.) Make notes on significant things you learned, new insights or understandings, questions that the readings raise.

Talk about your notes with someone in your small group or an adult Christian friend (small group counselor, youth director, pastor).

Reread Matthew 16:13-17. If you had been there, how would you have answered Jesus' question, "Who do you say that I am?"

- What are two specific ways your beliefs have changed over time?
- What caused the change?
- Are you growing more or less sure of what you believe about God, Jesus Christ?

Questioning is a natural and healthy part of growing faith during your teen years. Don't misinterpret your questioning to be a lack of faith. Asking questions is a way to test and develop your beliefs; it helps bring you into a dynamic and intimate relationship with God.

A creed is a statement of belief. Create a personal creed to express what you believe about Jesus Christ. You might create a drawing or painting, write a poem, compose a song or rewrite lyrics to a song you know, or write a statement of faith.

Relating to Parents

—Meredith Poe, 17
Charlotte, North Carolina

For teenagers, parents are definitely not the easiest people to get along with. Sometimes I feel shortchanged, because parents got their own commandment: "Honor your father and your mother . . ." (Exodus 20:12). It's hard to fulfill this commandment, when parents hurt your feelings or refuse to work harder to understand you. I know there are times when all of us want to throw in the towel and say to ourselves, "I get to leave when I'm 18, why am I worrying with these people now?"

As hard as it is sometimes to correct your mom every time she says "groovy" instead of the latest word for cool, give it all you've got. You only have one set of parents, and unfortunately they will only be with you for a finite length of time. God gave us our parents, but God also gave us to our parents. We are to take care of them when they need us, because they gave us the best gift of all: life. A parental relationship is something you may only experience a couple of times in your life—with your parents and with your own children. So take advantage of what you've got, and do your best to be the finest son or daughter ever. If you sometimes feel down about getting along with your parents, your heavenly Father will always be there to help you stay on track.

Although Jesus Christ is the center of our faith, he is rarely discussed outside of Sunday school lessons and sermons. Especially in school, talking about Jesus seems to be faux pas. It's not that young Christians deny him, it's just that many try to avoid the subject. This is unfortunate. Our entire religion is centered around the sacrifice of one man, yet so many of his followers find it difficult to talk openly about him, which is what makes Synago groups so great.

I believe that Jesus Christ sacrificed his own life so that I can live my life for him and him alone—not for anyone else, or any material possessions on this earth. I live with the confidence that Jesus has led the way for me to make a positive difference in people's lives. I do not fear, because through my faith in him I will not die when I leave this world, but have everlasting life at his side. This reassurance means a whole lot to me as a teenager who lives in today's world of violence and terrorism. Jesus is my ultimate trump card. No matter what situation I may face or stress I may be under, I know that Jesus was sent to save my soul, and that is all that matters.

It is so easy to be a Sunday Christian. The "holy" answers are the right answers at church, and no one is there to judge or shun you because of your "Jesus talk." Unfortunately, the outside world is not so kind. To stick up for Jesus, persons must often oppose the majority and open themselves up to questioning and ridicule. This is difficult for many who merely wish to fit in with the crowd and believe in Jesus whenever it is convenient for them. But Jesus did not teach us to take the easy way out. He went against the grain dozens of times. It is through my faith in him that I have the strength and confidence to do the same.

—Drew Harston, 18

Charlotte, North Carolina

Exodus 20:12 (NRSV)

"Honor your father and mother, so that your days may be long in the land that the LORD your God is giving you."

Ephesians 5:21, 6:1-4 (CEV)

Honor Christ and put others first. . . .

Children, you belong to the Lord, and you do the right thing when you obey your parents. The first commandment with a promise says, "Obey your father and your mother, and you will have a long and happy life."

Parents, don't be hard on your children. Raise them properly. Teach them and instruct them about the Lord.

John 19:25-27 (NIV)

Near the cross of Jesus stood his mother, his mother's sister, Mary the wife of Clopas, and Mary Magdalene. When Jesus saw his mother there, and the disciple whom he loved standing nearby, he said to his mother, "Dear woman, here is your son," and to the disciple, "Here is your mother." From that time on, this disciple took her into his home.

"Took her into his home" means "became responsible for her." In that culture a woman was dependent upon a father, husband, or son to provide for her.

"Honor" means "to respect, prize highly, care for, obey."

Exodus 20:12 is number five of the Ten Commandments (literally the "ten utterances"), rules of conduct given by God through Moses to the Hebrew people.

code of conduct in Ephesians 5:21-6:9 for spouses, parents and kids, and slaves nd masters helped ensure the running of a good household.

Notes

Pray for

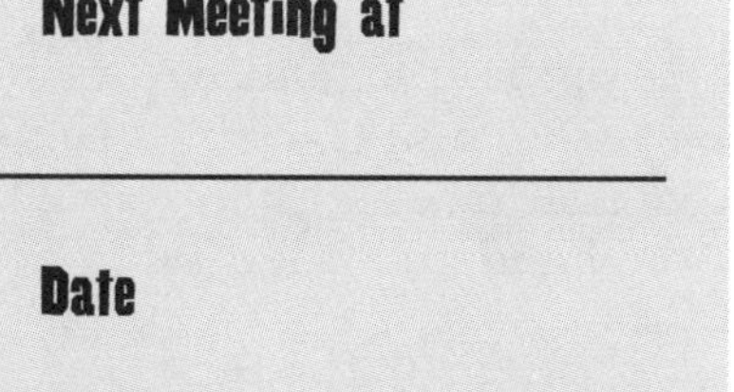
Next Meeting at

____

Date

____

parents. The earlier promise for the Hebrews was occupation of the "land" (Palestine); Paul's more general "long and happy life" made the promise more relevant for the Ephesians.

"The disciple whom he loved" refers to John.

R & R

REFLECT AND RESPOND

Read the biblical texts. Copy Exodus 20:12 onto several slips of paper and put them where you'll see them during the week: in your backpack, sock drawer, wallet, a book you're reading. During the week, think and pray about your relationship with your parents.

Draw a family tree of your family (adults you're related to or who are like family to you). Include parents, stepparents, guardians, grandparents, aunts, uncles, and other significant adults in your life. Circle those who are easy to respect. Put a box around those who are difficult to respect. Thank God for those you've circled. Tell God why it's difficult to honor the others, and ask for help to find ways to respect them. Pray for them by name.

Think about ways you honor your parents or guardians. List three things you do that honor them—and Christ. List three things you will try to change, with God's help.

Reread John 19:25a, 26-27. Close your eyes and imagine that Jesus is standing between you and your parents. He says to you, "These are your parents. Be responsible for them."

- How does that make you feel?
- What does it make you think?
- What actions will you take?

The disciples had cast out many demons (Mark 6:13) before failing to heal the demon-possessed boy. Jesus says that their failure was due to their lack of faith.

John 20:24-29 (NRSV)

But Thomas (who was called the Twin), one of the twelve, was not with them when Jesus came. So the other disciples told him, "We have seen the Lord." But he said to them, "Unless I see the mark of the nails in his hands, and put my finger in the mark of the nails and my hand in his side, I will not believe."

A week later his disciples were again in the house, and Thomas was with them. Although the doors were shut, Jesus came and stood among them and said, "Peace be with you." Then he said to Thomas, "Put your finger here and see my hands. Reach out your hand and put it in my side. Do not doubt but believe." Thomas answered him, "My Lord and my God!" Jesus said to him, "Have you believed because you have seen me? Blessed are those who have not seen and yet have come to believe."

Mark 9:17b-27 (NRSV)

"Teacher, I brought you my son; he has a spirit that makes him unable to speak; and whenever it seizes him, it dashes him down; and he foams and grinds his teeth and becomes rigid; and I asked your disciples to cast it out, but they could not do so." He answered them, "You faithless generation, how much longer must I be among you? How much longer must I put up with you? Bring him to me."

And they brought the boy to him. When the spirit saw [Jesus], immediately it convulsed the boy, and he fell on the ground and rolled about, foaming at the mouth. Jesus asked the father, "How long has this been happening?" And he said, "From childhood. It has often cast him into the fire and into the water, to destroy him; but if you are able to do anything, have pity on us and help us." Jesus said, "If you are able!—All things can be done for the one who believes."

Immediately the father of the child cried out, "I believe; help my unbelief!" . . .

[Jesus commanded] ". . . Come out of him, and never enter him again!" After crying out and convulsing him terribly, it came out, and the boy was like a corpse, so that most of them said, "He is dead." But Jesus took him by the hand and lifted him up, and he was able to stand.

Notes

Pray For

Next Meeting at

____

Date

____

R & R

REFLECT AND RESPOND

Read John 20:24-29 slowly, imagining the moods, actions, and dialogues of the people involved. Then do one of the following:

- Script a dialogue for the two scenes in the biblical text.
- Draw or paint how you see or interpret the story.
- Think of people you could imagine in the roles of Thomas and the disciples.

List songs or lyrics that capture what those in the story are feeling or trying to communicate.

Whom do you relate to more—Thomas or the other disciples?

If you relate to Thomas, complete this statement: "Unless I

______________________,

I will not believe."

- If you relate more to the disciples, how could you encourage a doubting friend who wants to believe?
- Jesus gave Thomas the proof he needed to remove his doubts. Can you trust Jesus to do that for you?

Read Mark 9:14-27, imagining the feelings and emotions of those in the story. What words would you use to describe:

the disciples

____

Jesus

____

the boy's father

____

Jesus' disciple Thomas was the original "doubting Thomas."

Calm in the Storm

The lake that Jesus and his disciples were crossing is known as the Sea of Galilee. Violent storms can occur suddenly when hot, humid air above the lake clashes with cool air from the Mediterranean Sea.

Matthew 14:22-33 (NIV)

Jesus made the disciples get into the boat and go on ahead of him to the other side [of the lake], while he dismissed the crowd. After he had dismissed them, he went up on a mountainside by himself to pray. When evening came, he was there alone, but the boat was already a considerable distance from land, buffeted by the waves because the wind was against it.

During the fourth watch of the night Jesus went out to them, walking on the lake. When the disciples saw him walking on the lake, they were terrified. "It's a ghost," they said, and cried out in fear.

But Jesus immediately said to them: "Take courage! It is I. Don't be afraid."

"Lord, if it's you," Peter replied, "tell me to come to you on the water."

"Come," he said.

Then Peter got down out of the boat, walked on the water and came toward Jesus. But when he saw the wind, he was afraid and, beginning to sink, cried out, "Lord, save me!"

Immediately Jesus reached out his hand and caught him. "You of little faith," he said, "why did you doubt?"

And when they climbed into the boat, the wind died down. Then those who were in the boat worshiped him, saying, "Truly you are the Son of God."

Mark 4:35-41 (NIV)

That day when evening came, he said to his disciples, "Let us go over to the other side [of the lake]." Leaving the crowd behind, they took him along, just as he was, in the boat. There were also other boats with him. A furious squall came up, and the waves broke over the boat, so that it was nearly swamped. Jesus was in the stern, sleeping on a cushion. The disciples woke him and said to him, "Teacher, don't you care if we drown?"

He got up, rebuked the wind and said to the waves, "Quiet! Be still!" Then the wind died down and it was completely calm.

He said to his disciples, "Why are you so afraid? Do you still have no faith?"

They were terrified and asked each other, "Who is this? Even the wind and the waves obey him!"

"Fourth watch" is the period of time from 3:00 A.M. to 6:00 A.M. The Romans divided the night into four watches, with the fourth being the la

Notes

Pray For

Next Meeting at

____

Date

____

R & R

REFLECT AND RESPOND

If your life were a weather map, what would it look like?

__ clear, sunny skies

__ sunny, chance of showers

__ partly cloudy

__ showers and thunderstorms

__ tornado warning

Read Matthew 14:22-33.

- If you were in the story, where would you be? Scared and huddled up on the boat? Hopping overboard to walk on water? In the water and sinking fast?

Read both passages.

- What do his words and actions tell you about: who he was? how he felt about the disciples? what he wanted to teach them?

When you encounter life's storms, imagine yourself in a boat with Christ, as the waves crash and the winds whip. Do as his disciples did:

- Wake him up. (How is your relationship with Christ? alive or sleeping?)
- Tell him about the storm. (Tell God what's going on. Admit your fears.)
- Stand back and watch. (Trust in the divine power. Let God work. Don't try to do something beyond your human capabilities.)
- Acknowledge and praise him with the disciples' words: "Even the winds and the waves obey him."

Closing Time

Matthew 18:20 (NRSV)

(Jesus is speaking to his disciples.)

"For where two or three are gathered in my name, I am there among them."

Acts 2:42, 44-47 (NRSV)

(The beginnings of the Christian church were small groups.)

They devoted themselves to the apostles' teaching and fellowship, to the breaking of bread and the prayers. . . .

All who believed were together and had all things in common; they would sell their possessions and goods and distribute the proceeds to all, as any had need. Day by day, as they spent much time together in the temple, they broke bread at home and ate their food with glad and generous hearts, praising God and having the goodwill of all the people. And day by day the Lord added to their number those who were being saved.

1 Thessalonians 5:11 (NRSV)

"Therefore encourage one another and build up each other, as indeed you are doing."

The "apostles' teaching" would have included all that Jesus himself taught, as well as the story and significance of his death, burial, and resurrection.

The apostle Paul wrote his letter to the Christian church in Thessaloni a busy seaport city, around 51 A.D. Paul wanted to encourage recent converts in the church, who had little external support in the generall pagan society.

ne definition of "fellowship" is "a gathering of believers as a corporate body for e purpose of worship."

Lord's Supper, following Jesus' teaching to "do this in remembrance" of him (Luke 22:19).

Notes

Pray for

Next Meeting at

____

Date

____

R & R

REFLECT AND RESPOND

Write your own description of "church." Then, read the first two biblical texts. How is your definition of church similar to what is described in these verses?

List the activities that characterized the church, as described in Acts.

- What drew people to become Christians and be part of the early church?
- Would those characteristics have the same effect today? Why, or why not?

List the faith communities you belong to (church, youth group, Synago small group, and so forth).

- On a scale of 1 to 10, rate how well each reflects the spirit and activities described in these passages, with 10 being "strongly reflects."
- As a member of a faith community (your church, Synago group, youth group, or other), what are three things you can do to help it become more like the early church?

Read 1 Thessalonians 5:1. Reflect on your small group experience. Look through your Notebook at the prayer lists and the notes you've made. Think of your experiences and the people who have blessed you, and say a prayer of thanks to God. Ask for God's guidance for your continued spiritual growth.

"Build up" is a phrase that literally referred to building houses but, Paul used it frequently to talk about growing in Christian character.

Group Members

Leader: ______________________ Phone ______________________

E-mail______________________

Leader: ______________________ Phone ______________________

E-mail______________________

Counselor: ______________________ Phone ______________________

E-mail______________________

Counselor: ______________________ Phone ______________________

e-mail ______________________

______________________ Phone: ______________________

Address:______________________

____

E-mail: ______________________

______________________ Phone: ______________________

Address:______________________

____

E-mail: ______________________

______________________ Phone: ______________________

Address:______________________

____

E-mail: ______________________

______________________ Phone: ______________________

Address:______________________

____

E-mail: ______________________

Phone:

Address:

E-mail:

Phone:

Address:

E-mail:

Phone:

Address:

E-mail:

Phone:

Address:

E-mail:

Phone:

Address:

E-mail:

Phone:

Address:

E-mail:

Phone:

Address:

E-mail:

SYNAGO

Synago (syn-AH-go) is the Greek word for "come together." It is the root word of "synagogue" a place were people come together to worship and to learn the life-giving faith. In Synago, you too will find a place among friends who come together to worship and to learn.

"Synago" also means "to take in." You know who's seeking, who's struggling, who's in need of God's love. Invite them, and let the Synago group take them in with love.

"Synago" is also the root word of "synergy," where the coming together of individual parts makes something even greater. And so it is in Synago. In coming together to talk about your lives in light of God's good news, you will find that something great happens.

Welcome to Synago.